CELEBRATING THE NAME ROBERT

Celebrating the Name Robert

Walter the Educator

Silent King Books a WhichHead imprint

Copyright © 2024 by Walter the Educator

All rights reserved. No part of this book may be reproduced in any manner whatsoever without written permission except in the case of brief quotations embodied in critical articles and reviews.

First Printing, 2024

Disclaimer
This book is a literary work; poems are not about specific persons, locations, situations, and/or circumstances unless mentioned in a historical context. This book is for entertainment and informational purposes only. The author and publisher offer this information without warranties expressed or implied. No matter the grounds, neither the author nor the publisher will be accountable for any losses, injuries, or other damages caused by the reader's use of this book. The use of this book acknowledges an understanding and acceptance of this disclaimer.

dedicated to everyone with the first name of Robert

CONTENTS

Dedication V

One - Forever Shine 1

Two - Toast To Robert's Name 3

Three - Echoes Strong 5

Four - Stands The Test Of Time 7

Five - Name So Grand 9

Six - Majestic 11

Seven - Legacy That Never Dies 13

Eight - Corner Of The Land 15

Nine - Like The Morning Sun 17

Ten - Tribute To Greatness 19

Eleven - Robert, Oh Robert 21

Twelve - Carved In Stone 23

Thirteen - Bold And True 25

Fourteen - Echoes Link	27
Fifteen - Eternally Bright	29
Sixteen - Forever Bright	31
Seventeen - Beautifully Erupted	33
Eighteen - Name To Remember	35
Nineteen - Boundless And Feathered	37
Twenty - Weaving Forever	39
Twenty-One - Robert Stands Tall	41
Twenty-Two - Rhythm So Divine	43
Twenty-Three - Forever In Our Soul	45
Twenty-Four - Beyond Compare	47
Twenty-Five - Let It Ring	49
Twenty-Six - Truly Infinite	51
Twenty-Seven - Forever Last	53
Twenty-Eight - Never Fade	55
Twenty-Nine - Proudly Wave	57
Thirty - Cherished Name	59
Thirty-One - Vibrant And True	61
Thirty-Two - Magic Fills The Air	63
Thirty-Three - Won't Forget	65

Thirty-Four - Resplendent Light 67

Thirty-Five - Elegance And Chance 69

About The Creator 71

ONE

FOREVER SHINE

In the realm of names, none quite compare
To the noble sound of Robert in the air
A moniker with regal strength and might
A name that shines with pure delight

Robert, a name with a history so grand
It echoes through time, a timeless brand
With syllables that dance upon the tongue
A melody of letters, ancient and young

From the rolling hills to the bustling town
The name of Robert wears a golden crown
It carries stories of courage and might
A beacon of hope in the darkest night

With each letter, a tale unfolds
Of bravery, honor, and stories untold
Ringing through the ages, a name so true
Robert, oh Robert, we celebrate you

In every corner of the world, the name is sung
A symphony of letters, each one finely strung
And as the stars illuminate the night
The name of Robert shines ever bright

So here's to Robert, a name so dear
A timeless treasure, crystal clear
In every verse and in every line
The name of Robert will forever shine

TWO

TOAST TO ROBERT'S NAME

Robert, a name of strength and might,
In battles fierce, you shine so bright,
A warrior's heart beats within your chest,
In dreams of glory, you never rest.

With words of wisdom, you guide the way,
Through darkest nights and brightest day,
A beacon of hope in times of despair,
Your kindness and courage, beyond compare.

R is for the resilience you possess,
O for the optimism you express,
B for the bravery that fills your soul,
E for the empathy that makes you whole,
R for the respect you give to all,
T for the truth in each word you call.

In forests deep and mountains high,

Your spirit soars into the sky,
With every step, you leave your mark,
A legacy that lights the dark.
    Robert, a name that echoes strong,
In history's tapestry, you belong,
Your story written in stars above,
A testament to your endless love.
    So raise a toast to Robert's name,
A symphony of honor, acclaim,
May his name forever resound,
In every corner, on every ground.

THREE

ECHOES STRONG

Robert, a name that dances on the wind,
A melody of strength and wisdom combined,
In forests deep and meadows wide,
Your spirit roams, a fearless guide.
With a heart of gold and a mind so keen,
In every challenge, you reign supreme,
A leader born, with courage ablaze,
In every step, you light the ways.
Beneath the stars, your dreams take flight,
A symphony of hope, burning bright,
In every tale, your legend grows,
A legacy that forever flows.
R is for the resilience you possess,
O for the optimism you caress,
B for the bravery that fuels your fire,
E for the empathy that never tires,

R for the respect you freely give,
T for the truth in how you live.

In every smile and every tear,
Your presence soothes, dispelling fear,
A gentle soul with a lion's roar,
In every storm, you seek for more.

So here's to Robert, a name so grand,
A champion in every land,
May your spirit soar, forever free,
A beacon of hope for all to see.

Robert, a name that echoes strong,
In history's tale, you surely belong,
Your story etched in time's embrace,
A tribute to your enduring grace.

FOUR

STANDS THE TEST OF TIME

Robert, a name that echoes through the ages,
In every line of history's pages,
A symphony of strength and noble grace,
In every challenge, you boldly embrace.

With each sunrise, your spirit soars,
A beacon of hope, an open door,
In every heart, your kindness blooms,
A sanctuary amid life's fumes.

R is for the resilience you display,
O for the optimism that lights your way,
B for the bravery that fuels your soul,
E for the empathy that makes you whole,
R for the reverence in all you do,
T for the truth that shines from you.

In every mountain and valley low,

Your courage flows, a steady flow,
In every forest and city street,
Your presence lingers, strong and sweet.

With every word, a tale unfolds,
Of a warrior's spirit, brave and bold,
In every silence, your wisdom speaks,
A melody that every heart seeks.

So here's to Robert, a name so true,
A champion in all that you pursue,
May your legacy forever stand,
A testament to your guiding hand.

Robert, a name that stands the test of time,
In every journey, you brightly shine,
Your story woven in the stars above,
A celebration of your boundless love.

FIVE

NAME SO GRAND

In the realm of names, there's one that reigns supreme
A name that echoes through time like a vibrant dream
Robert, a moniker with a regal air
A title that shines with an illustrious flair
From ancient lands to modern days
Robert's legacy forever sways
A name that carries strength and grace
A timeless emblem, a noble embrace
In the tapestry of names, Robert stands tall
Like a towering oak, steadfast and overall
With syllables that dance upon the tongue
A symphony of letters, from which songs are sung
From Robin Hood to Robert Frost
Legends and poets, a name embossed

In the annals of history, Robert's tale
A name that will forever prevail
    Oh, Robert, a name that commands respect
A beacon of honor, a name we never neglect
In every Robert, a story unfolds
A narrative of courage, a saga untold
    So let us raise our voices high
And sing the praises of Robert, nigh
For in this name, we find allure
A name so grand, so noble, so pure

SIX

MAJESTIC

In the realm of names, a gem so rare
Robert, a symphony beyond compare
A name that echoes through time and space
With dignity and grace, it holds its place
From ancient courts to modern streets
Robert's legacy forever beats
A name that carries tales of might
A beacon of valor, a gallant knight
In the tapestry of names, Robert stands tall
A titan of letters, captivating all
With a rhythm that dances on the ear
A melody of honor, so crystal clear
From Robert Burns to Robert Kennedy
A name that resonates with history
In the annals of time, Robert's tale prevails
A legacy of courage, a saga that never fails

    Oh, Robert, a name of noble renown
A symposium of honor, wearing a crown
In every Robert, a legend unfurls
A narrative of triumph, a banner that swirls
    So let us raise our voices in acclaim
And celebrate the name of Robert, aflame
For in this name, a story is told
A name so majestic, so gallant, so bold

SEVEN

LEGACY THAT NEVER DIES

In realms of old, where tales unfold
There lived a man, both brave and bold
His name was Robert, a name of might
A gallant soul, with heart alight
In fields of green, he roamed so free
With every step, a symphony
His laughter rang like silver bells
And in his eyes, a thousand spells
Robert, the warrior with a lion's heart
His valor shining, a work of art
He marched through storms, with steadfast grace
In every trial, he found his place
In dreams, he soared on wings of gold
His spirit bright, a sight to behold

With every word, a melody
His name, a song for all to see
    So let us raise our voices high
And sing the praise of Robert nigh
For in this name, a legend lies
A legacy that never dies

EIGHT

CORNER OF THE LAND

Of noble birth and steady heart,
In tales of old, he plays a part,
Robert, a name that stands with pride,
In every field, he will abide.

With courage strong and spirit bold,
In every story, he's been told,
Robert, a name that echoes far,
Like a shining, guiding star.

In every land, in every tongue,
His name is sung, his deeds are sung,
Robert, a name that holds its sway,
In every night and brightened day.

In fields of battle, he does stand,
A valiant knight with sword in hand,

Robert, a name that rings out loud,
In every valiant, valiant crowd.
   In halls of wisdom, he does speak,
With knowledge vast and wisdom meek,
Robert, a name that holds its own,
In every land that's ever known.
   So raise a glass, and sing his name,
Let it echo in the hall of fame,
Robert, a name that's truly grand,
In every corner of the land.

NINE

LIKE THE MORNING SUN

In the realm of names, there's one that reigns supreme
A moniker of strength, a nobleman's dream
Robert, oh Robert, your syllables ring
With power and grace, like a mighty king
    Your consonants clash in a symphony bold
A warrior's anthem, a tale untold
The R rolls like thunder, the B stands strong
O and E, a dance, a melodious song
    In ancient lore, your name carries weight
A hero's title, a knight so great
In modern times, you stand with pride
A timeless classic, never to hide
    Robert, oh Robert, a name so grand
Echoes of history, across the land

From castles and courts to city streets
Your legacy lives, never retreats
    So here's to you, Robert, a name of might
A beacon of courage, a guiding light
In every syllable, a story untold
In every letter, a legend unfolds
    Robert, oh Robert, your name we raise
In poetry and prose, in endless praise
For in this world, and the next to come
Your name shall shine, like the morning sun

TEN

TRIBUTE TO GREATNESS

    In the tapestry of names, one stands tall
A symphony of letters, a regal call
Robert, oh Robert, your essence shines bright
A constellation of sounds, a celestial flight
    The R resounds like a trumpet's blare
O and B dance, a cosmic affair
E and R weave a tale untold
Tethered to history, a name to behold
    In the annals of time, your presence is felt
A beacon of honor, in hearts deeply dwelt
From ancient valor to modern grace
Robert, oh Robert, you hold your place
    In gardens of language, you bloom and grow
A melody of syllables, a river's flow

Your resonance lingers in whispered air
A name so timeless, beyond compare
    Robert, oh Robert, a name to extol
In whispered prayers, in stories untold
From cradle to grave, in every heartbeat
Your name echoes on, a rhythm so sweet
    So here's to you, Robert, in prose and rhyme
A tribute to greatness, throughout all time
In every echo, in every word
Your name resounds, like a songbird.

ELEVEN

ROBERT, OH ROBERT

In the tapestry of names, one shines bright
A symphony of letters, a beacon of light
Robert, oh Robert, a name of renown
In every syllable, a regal crown
    The R rolls like thunder, a warrior's call
O and B dance, in harmony enthrall
E and R, a melody divine
In every utterance, a tale to enshrine
    In history's embrace, your name stands tall
A titan of honor, in legends that enthrall
From courtly splendor to humble abode
Robert, oh Robert, a name to uphold
    In the lexicon of life, your presence resounds
A symposium of strength, in echoes unbound
From ancient lineage to modern day
Robert, oh Robert, in every way

    In the annals of time, your legacy gleams
A constellation of letters, a poet's dreams
In every verse, in every line
Your name lingers on, a treasure so fine
    So here's to you, Robert, in prose and song
A testament to greatness, enduring and strong
In every heartbeat, in every word
Your name prevails, like a soaring bird.

TWELVE

CARVED IN STONE

In the realm of names, there's one that reigns,
A moniker that holds its own, and never wanes.
Robert, oh Robert, a name so strong and true,
It echoes through the ages, a timeless debut.

With syllables that dance and letters that entwine,
Robert, oh Robert, a name so divine.
From the rolling hills to the bustling city streets,
The name Robert resonates, never facing defeat.

In the tapestry of names, it stands bold and bright,
A beacon of strength, a guiding light.
From Robert the Bruce to Robert Frost,
This name has never been at a loss.

In every consonant and every vowel,
Robert, oh Robert, a name that towers like a castle's tall outer wall.
It weaves through history, a thread of valor and might,

A name that commands respect, even in the darkest night.
  So here's to Robert, a name to be revered,
A symphony of letters, a name to be cheered.
In every corner of the earth, let it be known,
Robert, oh Robert, a name that's carved in stone.

THIRTEEN

BOLD AND TRUE

In the grand tapestry of names, one shines bright,
With a regal charm that ignites the night.
Robert, oh Robert, a name that stands tall,
A symphony of letters, never to fall.

From the ancient halls to the modern streets,
Robert, oh Robert, a name that beats.
Like a melody that lingers in the air,
It holds a timeless elegance, beyond compare.

In the whispers of the wind and the laughter of the stream,
The name Robert echoes like a beautiful dream.
It carries the weight of history and the promise of tomorrow,
A name that weaves together joy and sorrow.

In the depths of its syllables, there lies a tale,
Of bravery, honor, and a spirit that will prevail.

From Robert Burns to Robert Kennedy,
This name has left its mark through centuries of history.
  So here's to Robert, a name that's bold and true,
A beacon of strength in all that it will do.
In every corner of the world, let it resound,
Robert, oh Robert, a name that knows no bound.

FOURTEEN

ECHOES LINK

In realms where echoes dance with light,
A name emerges, bold and bright.
Robert, a symphony of strength,
In life's grand tapestry, we find the length.
 Beneath the moon's enchanting glow,
Robert's essence begins to grow.
A beacon in the vast unknown,
A name by destiny finely sown.
 Through valleys deep and mountains high,
Robert's spirit, like a falcon, shall fly.
In whispers of the gentle breeze,
A tale of resilience it decrees.
 Majestic as the oak tree's embrace,
Robert's name, a sanctuary in grace.
In every sunrise, a new chapter unfolds,
With Robert's legacy, the story molds.

With courage in the face of the night,
Robert's name, a guiding light.
A tapestry woven with threads divine,
In the cosmic anthology, it does shine.

Oh, Robert, a melody in time,
In every stanza, your name does chime.
A sonnet written in celestial ink,
In the vast expanse, your echoes link.

FIFTEEN

ETERNALLY BRIGHT

In the realm of echoes and cosmic delight,
Resides a name that sparkles in the night.
Robert, a symphony of celestial hues,
A melody that the universe happily strews.

Beneath the constellations, Robert gleams,
A celestial poet in astral dreams.
In the celestial tapestry, his name unfurls,
A constellation of wisdom that time swirls.

Amidst the galaxies, a comet's grace,
Robert's name dances, leaving a trace.
A cosmic dance in the cosmic ballet,
In the stellar waltz, he finds his way.

Within the aurora's vibrant embrace,
Robert's essence, a celestial grace.
A comet carving stories in the cosmic scroll,
In the grand celestial theatre, he plays a role.

    Through the nebulae's swirling mist,
Robert's name, a celestial tryst.
A celestial sonnet sung by the stars,
In the cosmic ballad, he leaves memoirs.
    Oh, Robert, in the astral sea,
A celestial voyage, forever free.
In the cosmic sonnet, your name's delight,
A celestial symphony, eternally bright.

SIXTEEN

FOREVER BRIGHT

In the tapestry of time, a name unfolds,
Robert, a story that the universe holds.
Beyond the realms where galaxies soar,
A celestial hymn, forevermore.
    Beneath the arches of the cosmic dome,
Robert's name, a kaleidoscope poem.
In the stellar dance of night and day,
A cosmic melody in the astral ballet.
    Among the stars, a comet's grace,
Robert's essence, a cosmic embrace.
A luminary journey in the cosmic sea,
In celestial realms, he's forever free.
    Through the whispers of the cosmic wind,
Robert's legacy, a tale thinned.

A constellation etched in cosmic lore,
In the vast cosmos, forevermore.
    Within the nebula's vibrant embrace,
Robert's name, a celestial trace.
A comet carving arcs in the astral scroll,
In cosmic whispers, stories extol.
    Oh, Robert, in the cosmic expanse,
A celestial dance, a cosmic chance.
In the cosmic sonnet of eternal night,
Your name echoes, forever bright.

SEVENTEEN

BEAUTIFULLY ERUPTED

In the realm of names, a beacon brightly shines,
Robert, a moniker that gracefully twines.
Echoes of strength in syllables woven,
A resolute melody through time, unbroken.
    Bearing a legacy, noble and grand,
In the poetic symphony, a name to withstand.
Robust as the oak, steadfast and true,
In the garden of names, a perennial hue.
    Robust Robert, with each letter enlaced,
A harmonic resonance, a name embraced.
In linguistic realms, a majestic decree,
A linguistic voyage, a captivating sea.
    Rapturous echoes in the whispers of fate,
Robert, a name that none underrate.

Crafted in letters, a lyrical dance,
A timeless sonnet, a celestial trance.
  Riding the waves of linguistic art,
In the tapestry of names, a masterpiece to impart.
Robert, a symphony, uniquely spun,
In the lexicon's gallery, a radiant sun.
  So let the verses unfold, an ode to thee,
Robert, a name adorned in eternity.
In the mosaic of words, a masterpiece sculpted,
A poetic celebration, beautifully erupted.

EIGHTEEN

NAME TO REMEMBER

Amidst the tapestry of nomenclature's vast array,
Robert emerges, a gem in the lexicon's ballet.
Not merely letters entwined in mundane array,
But a rhythmic cadence, a linguistic ballet.

Robert, a symphony sung by celestial quills,
Echoes in verses, among linguistic hills.
Not just a name, but a voyage profound,
In the vast sea of lexemes, a treasure found.

A symphony of consonants, a dance of vowels,
In the realm of names, where uniqueness prowls.
Each syllable, a brushstroke on language's canvas,
Crafting a portrait, in the lexicon's expanse.

In the garden of appellations, Robert stands tall,
A melodic resonance, a clarion call.
No mere label, but a lyrical revelation,
In the poetic orchestra, a jubilation.

With each letter, a narrative unfolds,
A saga of echoes, in verses it molds.
Robert, not just a tag, but a poetic decree,
A kaleidoscope of words, an artistry.
So let the linguistic ballad serenade,
Robert, a name, in beauty arrayed.
In the anthology of words, a radiant ember,
A lyrical celebration, a name to remember.

NINETEEN

BOUNDLESS AND FEATHERED

Beneath the cosmic canopy, a name takes flight,
Robert, a constellation in language's boundless night.
Not a mere utterance, but a celestial spark,
In the galaxy of names, leaving a luminous mark.

In the symphony of syllables, a melodic grace,
Robert, a harmonious echo in time and space.
Not confined to letters, but a linguistic art,
A masterpiece woven, an intricate part.

Each vowel and consonant, a cosmic dance,
In the cosmic ballet, a linguistic trance.
Robert, not just a label, but a cosmic decree,
A stellar composition, an ode to eternity.

In the lexicon's cosmos, a stellar parade,
Robert, a celestial journey, not to fade.

Beyond earthly confines, in celestial scope,
A radiant name, an ethereal trope.
   In the celestial atlas, where words align,
Robert, a constellation, forever to shine.
Not just a name, but a cosmic ballet,
In the cosmic poem, a star-studded display.
   So let the verses cascade, a cosmic rhyme,
Robert, a celestial name, transcending time.
In the astral sonnet, a celestial tether,
A poetic celebration, boundless and feathered.

TWENTY

WEAVING FOREVER

In the tapestry of language, a jewel unfurls,
Robert, a symphony of letters that swirls.
Not a mere tag, but an ode to the soul,
In the lexicon's embrace, a name to extol.

A linguistic voyage, a poetic cascade,
In the lyrical labyrinth, where echoes evade.
Robert, not confined to mere phonetic frame,
A kaleidoscope of syllables, a linguistic flame.

Each consonant, a brushstroke in the art,
A masterpiece of letters, a poetic chart.
In the gallery of names, Robert stands bold,
A vibrant sonnet, an epic untold.

Beyond the mundane, in linguistic delight,
Robert, a constellation in the poet's night.

Not just a name, but a lyrical spree,
A ballad of letters, a jubilant decree.
    With resonance profound, in the heart it rings,
In the lexicon's ballroom, where melody springs.
Robert, not a label, but a poetic ember,
A harmonious celebration, an eternal member.
    So let the verses unfurl, a linguistic sea,
Robert, a name, in its own symphony.
In the poetic anthology, a timeless tether,
A euphonic celebration, weaving forever.

TWENTY-ONE

ROBERT STANDS TALL

In the realm of names, Robert stands tall,
A linguistic tapestry, a lyrical sprawl.
Not just syllables, but a poetic spree,
In the lexicon's garden, a jubilant glee.

Each letter, a brushstroke in the canvas of sound,
Robert, a melodic echo, profound.
Not confined to labels, but a poetic decree,
A sonnet of letters, in language's sea.

A symphony of consonants, a dance of rhyme,
In the poetic ballroom, through space and time.
Robert, a name that gracefully weaves,
A celestial sonnet, a treasure it leaves.

Beyond phonetics, in the essence it dwells,
A poetic journey, where eloquence swells.
Not just a tag, but a lyrical embrace,
In the poetic realm, a timeless grace.

With each syllable, a story unfolds,
Robert, a narrative, in letters it molds.
In the lexicon's sonnet, a vibrant hue,
A linguistic celebration, forever true.

So let the verses dance, a lyrical flight,
Robert, a name, in the poet's light.
In the anthology of words, a radiant ember,
A poetic symphony, eternally remember.

TWENTY-TWO

RHYTHM SO DIVINE

In the realm of names, Robert stands tall and true
A moniker of strength, of honor, and virtue
With syllables that dance and letters that sing
A name that echoes through the ages, an everlasting thing

From Robin Hood to Robert Frost
This name has carried legends, never lost
In tales of bravery and words of wisdom
Robert's presence shines, never to be outdone

From the rolling hills to the bustling streets
The name of Robert, a melody that repeats
Like a symphony, rich and bold
A name that never ceases to unfold

In every letter, a story to be told
In every sound, a legacy to uphold

So let us raise our voices high
And sing the praises of Robert, reaching for the sky
    For in this name, a universe resides
With endless possibilities, where dreams collide
So let us honor Robert, in all his glory
A name that holds within it, an extraordinary story
    From the beginning to the end of time
The name of Robert, a rhythm so divine
So let us cherish, let us adore
The name of Robert, forevermore

TWENTY-THREE

FOREVER IN OUR SOUL

In the tapestry of names, Robert weaves a tale
A symphony of syllables, a song beyond the pale
A name that whispers of resilience and might
A beacon of strength, a guiding light
From ancient castles to modern streets
The name of Robert, a melody that repeats
In every echo, a legacy unfolds
In every heartbeat, a story untold
From Robert the Bruce to Robert Burns
This name has kindled fires, and bridges it churns
In the annals of history, it stands tall
A name that echoes through time's great hall
In each letter, a saga is inscribed
In each verse, a legend is described

So let us raise our voices, let us cheer
For the name of Robert, resounding and clear
    In every Robert, a universe resides
With dreams to chase and nowhere to hide
So let us honor Robert, in all his glory
A name that weaves an extraordinary story
    From dawn's first light to twilight's glow
The name of Robert, an anthem to bestow
So let us cherish, let us extol
The name of Robert, forever in our soul

TWENTY-FOUR

BEYOND COMPARE

In the realm of names, there's one that stands tall,
A moniker robust, it's Robert for all.
With strength and grace, it conquers the land,
A name so grand, it's truly grand.

Robert, oh Robert, a name so divine,
In history and lore, it continues to shine.
From kings to poets, it has left its mark,
A name of power, both light and dark.

In the echoes of time, it resonates strong,
A name that's enduring, where it truly belongs.
With syllables that dance and letters that sing,
Robert, oh Robert, a name fit for a king.

From the hills of Scotland to the streets of Rome,
This name has journeyed, a name to call home.
In every corner of the earth, its presence is felt,
A name of honor, where hearts will melt.

So raise a glass to Robert, let's toast and cheer,
For a name so renowned, so noble and dear.
In the tapestry of names, it's a masterpiece rare,
Robert, oh Robert, a name beyond compare.

TWENTY-FIVE

LET IT RING

Behold the name Robert, a melody so sweet,
In the symphony of names, it takes the lead seat.
With consonants and vowels, it weaves a tale,
A name that's timeless, it will never pale.

Robert, oh Robert, a name of might,
In the realm of titles, it shines so bright.
From ancient courts to modern streets,
It's a name that echoes, with every beat.

In the chambers of history, it stands tall,
A name of valor, it will never fall.
From knights to scholars, it's been embraced,
A name of honor, with no trace of waste.

With each letter dancing, in perfect array,
Robert, oh Robert, it's here to stay.
In the whispers of wind and the hum of the sea,
This name resounds, so wild and free.

So raise your voice for Robert, let it ring,
For a name so regal, like a crown for a king.
In the tapestry of names, it holds its own,
Robert, oh Robert, a name that's carved in stone.

TWENTY-SIX

TRULY INFINITE

In the realm of names, there's one that shines,
A moniker of strength, where greatness aligns.
Robert, O Robert, like a knight in the night,
Your name echoes with valor, a beacon of light.

From the ancient times to the modern age,
Robert has stood tall on history's stage.
A name with a rhythm, a melody divine,
In every syllable, a story to enshrine.

In the fields of battle, Robert stands strong,
A warrior's name, where courage belongs.
But beyond the armor, beneath the shield,
Lies a heart of gold, a spirit unconcealed.

Robert, the name that resonates with power,
A symphony of letters in a timeless tower.
In every consonant, in every vowel,
Lies a legacy, a tale to howl.

From the whispers of the wind to the roaring sea,
Robert's name echoes through eternity.
It's a name of honor, a name of might,
A name that soars like an eagle in flight.
   So let us raise our voices, let us sing,
Of the name Robert, like a royal ring.
For in this world, there's no name quite like it,
A name that shines, a name that's truly infinite.

TWENTY-SEVEN

FOREVER LAST

In the realm of names, there lies a gem
A moniker grand, it's Robert, and then
With regal resonance, it rings so clear
A name that echoes through the atmosphere
Robert, a name of strength and might
A beacon of valor, a guiding light
In the tapestry of time, it stands secure
A name that's noble, steadfast, and pure
From ancient kings to modern days
Robert's legacy forever stays
A name that carries tales untold
Of chivalry, bravery, and stories bold
With syllables that dance upon the tongue
Robert, a name that's never unsung
It conjures images of grandeur and grace
A name that time and space can't erase

So let us raise a toast, a heartfelt cheer
For Robert, a name that's ever dear
In letters and sounds, it holds its place
A name that embodies strength and grace
    Oh, Robert, your name we celebrate
With verses and rhymes, we elevate
For in this world, there's no name quite like
Yours, Robert, a beacon shining bright
    So let the world resound with Robert's name
A symphony of letters, a timeless flame
For in this tapestry of names so vast
Robert, your name will forever last

TWENTY-EIGHT

NEVER FADE

Of noble birth, a name so strong,
Robert, a title that belongs,
To those with courage, brave and true,
In every heart, a fire that grew.
A name that echoes through the years,
Bringing hope and calming fears,
A beacon in the darkest night,
Guiding souls towards the light.
Robert, a symphony of power,
In every triumph, every hour,
A melody of strength and might,
A name that shines in the moon's soft light.
In every battle, in every quest,
Robert stands above the rest,
A name that speaks of honor and grace,
A legacy no time can erase.

From ancient lands to modern days,
Robert's name forever stays,
A testament to valor and might,
A symbol of unyielding fight.

So raise a glass and sing his praise,
For Robert's name will never fade,
In every heart, in every land,
A name that's truly grand.

In every story, every song,
Robert's legacy lives on,
A name that's etched in history's tome,
A name that will forever roam.

TWENTY-NINE

PROUDLY WAVE

In realms of old and tales untold,
There lived a name, a story to behold,
Robert, a name of ancient lore,
A name that echoes forevermore.

A name that carries a regal air,
A name that none can help but share,
In every realm, in every land,
Robert's name stands firm and grand.

From castle walls to mountain peaks,
Robert's name soars, it never weakens,
In every heart, a song it sings,
A name of warriors and mighty kings.

In whispers carried by the wind,
Robert's legacy will never rescind,
A name of honor, a name of might,
A beacon in the darkest night.

In every battle, in every fray,
Robert's name leads the way,
A name that speaks of courage and gall,
A name that one cannot but recall.

So let the banners proudly wave,
For Robert's name, so bold and brave,
In every tale, in every verse,
Robert's name will never disperse.

In every heart, in every soul,
Robert's name will forever extol,
A name that shines through history's tome,
A name that will forever roam.

THIRTY

CHERISHED NAME

In realms where stars entwine the night,
A name resounds with noble might.
Oh, Robert, beacon of renown,
Your essence, a laurel-woven crown.

In echoes of the ages past,
A melody, Robert, unsurpassed.
Through fields of time, your name persists,
A symphony of existence it insists.

Beneath the moon's enchanting glow,
Robert, thy legacy does grow.
Each syllable, a whispered ode,
In nature's script, a timeless code.

Within the tapestry of fate,
Robert, your presence, ever great.
Majestic as a mountain's peak,
In every verse, your spirit speaks.

A river winding through the years,
Robert, bearer of hopes and fears.
In every heartbeat, a rhythmic beat,
A sonnet written, ever sweet.
   So here's to you, in prose and rhyme,
Robert, enduring through the sands of time.
In the cosmic dance, a cherished name,
A beacon bright, forever aflame.

THIRTY-ONE

VIBRANT AND TRUE

In the realm where echoes dance and play,
Resides a name, Robert, like sunlit array.
Not mere letters strung in routine,
But a melody, a lyric, a celestial sheen.

Robert, the architect of dawn's embrace,
In syllables whispered, a timeless grace.
Through the labyrinth of language, you weave,
A sonnet of essence that hearts believe.

Amidst the garden of names, you stand,
Robert, like a painter's masterful hand.
Each consonant, a stroke of art,
A masterpiece etched on life's chart.

Beneath the tapestry of cosmic design,
Robert, a star in the vast celestial line.
A phoenix rising in the poetic sky,
In your name, dreams and realities tie.

    Not just a label, but a symphony's note,
Robert, in verses, your presence devote.
With each utterance, a spell you cast,
A legacy in time that forever will last.
    So here's to Robert, in prose anew,
A kaleidoscope of hues, vibrant and true.
In the lexicon of life, a radiant flame,
A timeless echo, Robert, your name.

THIRTY-TWO

MAGIC FILLS THE AIR

In realms where echoes dance, a name unfolds,
Robert, a symphony in letters bold.
A timeless melody, a whisper in the breeze,
In the tapestry of life, a thread that never sees release.

Beneath the moon's gentle glow, Robert's grace,
A celestial dance in the cosmic space.
Stars align to spell his name, celestial art,
A constellation's homage, a masterpiece's start.

Through valleys of time, where memories bloom,
Robert, a flower in eternity's perfume.
With every sunrise, a new chapter's birth,
In the canvas of existence, his name, a cherished mirth.

In the heart's secret garden, a whispering stream,
Robert, the muse of dreams, a tranquil gleam.

A phoenix rising, resilient and strong,
In the tapestry of destiny, his name, a vibrant song.
    Majestic mountains bow to his essence's might,
Robert, a beacon in the serene night.
In the cosmic dance, a celestial waltz,
His name, a verse in the universe's exalted halls.
    So let the quill dance, and the ink take flight,
In celebration of Robert, in the realm of poetic light.
A tapestry woven with words unique and rare,
For in the name of Robert, magic fills the air.

THIRTY-THREE

WON'T FORGET

In the symphony of syllables, where verses weave,
Robert, a poetic harmony, the soul's reprieve.
A name that resonates like autumn's rustling leaves,
In the poetic sonnet, where every heart believes.
 Through the corridors of time, where echoes linger,
Robert, a timeless echo, a storyteller's singer.
A narrative woven with threads of resilience,
In the grand tapestry, his name, a brilliance.
 Beneath the canvas of the night, a cosmic dance,
Robert, a starlight sonata, an astral trance.
Celestial notes in the galaxy's grand score,
His name, a constellation forevermore.
 Within the garden of words, where meanings bloom,
Robert, a linguistic blossom, dispelling gloom.

Syllabic petals in the linguistic meadow,
His name, a poetic breeze that continues to billow.
    Amidst the whispers of zephyrs, soft and low,
Robert, a serenade that continues to grow.
A melodic whisper in the wind's embrace,
His name, an anthem in the realm of grace.
    So let the quill dance, a pen's pirouette,
In honor of Robert, a name we won't forget.

THIRTY-FOUR

RESPLENDENT LIGHT

In the realm of names, a beacon bright,
Robert emerges with resplendent light.
A symphony of syllables, a melodic grace,
Echoing through time, leaving a lasting trace.

In letters woven, a tapestry of might,
Each curve, each consonant, a celestial flight.
Robert, a rhapsody in linguistic art,
A masterpiece carved into language's heart.

Beneath the moon's enchanting glow,
Robert dances in a rhythmic flow.
A name that echoes through the ages,
In history's book, it elegantly engages.

A titan of letters, a linguistic king,
In the poetry of names, a celestial wing.
Robert, a symphony of consonants and vowels,
In the lexicon's garden, it eternally prowls.

Celebrate the resonance, the linguistic bliss,
In the vast tapestry of names, Robert is a kiss.
A sonnet woven with linguistic delight,
Robert, a name that shines so bright.

THIRTY-FIVE

ELEGANCE AND CHANCE

In the realm of appellations, behold Robert's domain,
A moniker of strength, an eloquent refrain.
With syllabic cadence, a lyrical spell,
In the lexicon's embrace, it gallantly dwells.

Robert, a phoenix rising in linguistic flight,
A name that echoes through day and night.
Consonants and vowels, a harmonious blend,
In the vast symphony of names, it transcends.

A linguistic tapestry, woven with care,
In the grand narrative, Robert's name is rare.
Each letter, a brushstroke, on language's canvas,
A melodic sonnet, in poetic excess.

Through corridors of time, Robert strides,
A name that in history's embrace abides.

Majestic resonance in each syllable's grace,
In the annals of names, it finds its place.
    Celebrate the resonance, the alphabetic dance,
Robert, a name with elegance and chance.
A sonnet crafted with lexical delight,
In the mosaic of names, it gleams so bright.

ABOUT THE CREATOR

Walter the Educator is one of the pseudonyms for Walter Anderson. Formally educated in Chemistry, Business, and Education, he is an educator, an author, a diverse entrepreneur, and he is the son of a disabled war veteran. "Walter the Educator" shares his time between educating and creating. He holds interests and owns several creative projects that entertain, enlighten, enhance, and educate, hoping to inspire and motivate you.

Follow, find new works, and stay up to date
with Walter the Educator™
at WaltertheEducator.com

www.ingramcontent.com/pod-product-compliance
Lightning Source LLC
LaVergne TN
LVHW052000060526
838201LV00059B/3758